5/21/6

3 9082 11275 4711

D0055818

COSMOgirl cool room

35 make-it-yourself projects

Mark Montano

COSMOgirl cool room

35 make-it-yourself projects

Mark Montano

HEARST BOOKS
A division of Sterling Publishing Co., Inc.

New York / London
www.sterlingpublishing.com

Book design by Margaret Rubiano

Library of Congress Cataloging-in-Publication Data is on file for this title

10 9 8 7 6 5 4 3 2 1

Published by Hearst Books
A Division of Sterling Publishing Co., Inc.
387 Park Avenue South, New York, NY 10016

CosmoGIRL and Hearst Books are trademarks of Hearst Communications, Inc.

www.cosmogirl.com

For information about custom editions, special sales, premium and corporate
purchases, please contact Sterling Special Sales Department at 800-805-5489
or specialsales@sterlingpub.com.

Distributed in Canada by Sterling Publishing
c/o Canadian Manda Group, 165 Dufferin Street
Toronto, Ontario, Canada M6K 3H6

Distributed in Australia by Capricorn Link (Australia) Pty. Ltd.
P.O. Box 704, Windsor, NSW 2756 Australia

Manufactured in China

Sterling ISBN 978-1-58816-742-2

contents

susan's note

We know you love to be out in the world, but isn't it great to come home to a room you love? It's your sanctuary—the place to pop in the ear buds, curl up with the latest issue of *CosmoGirl*, and get away from it all. It's also the place to hang out with your friends, hold a sleepover, do your homework, roll out your yoga mat—and just be yourself.

All the more reason for your room to reflect you—your style, your interests, your personality. *CosmoGirl*'s very own decorating guru, Mark Montano, has been helping you realize your dream rooms for years. And now we've gathered the very best of Mark's ideas and techniques in one very cool guide.

Whether you like to surround yourself with royal luxury or a pop-art color scheme, you'll find something you like. More importantly, I know you'll take all these great ideas and give them a spin of your very own.

I can't wait to see all of your cool rooms, CosmoGirls. Email me anytime at **susan@cosmogirl.com.**

Love,

Susan

a few words from mark

The book you have in your hands has been a labor of love for many people. Not only does each room reflect the person who resides in it, but many people had a hand in making each room happen. Editors, shoppers, painters—and most of all *CosmoGirl* magazine. They allowed me to let my imagination run wild, designing rooms that would inspire girls like you from all over the world to recreate for themselves.

It all started in 1999, when I was asked to write a column that would show all of you how to make your rooms wonderful. "Cool Room" was the result, and over the following years we managed to come up with some fantastic living spaces just for you—everything from space-age designs to Moroccan themes. We had a blast thinking up fun things to do and showing you how to paint, where to shop, what was comfortable, what worked—and what didn't.   It was a great adventure!

The response was great. After a few columns, you began to email me—sometimes at a rate of 1000 per month!—with questions that ranged from where did you find that fabric to how did you hang that photo? I answered you all, no matter how long it took.

"Cool Room" helped me take my own career to new levels and eventually I was hired to be a designer on TLC's *While You Were Out*. What a great experience that was! And I think the TV show made me a better contributing editor to *CosmoGirl*—we even featured a *While-You-Were-Out* room in the magazine.

I truly believe that your room should be a reflection of who you are. It should be your safe space where you feel the most comfortable, sleep like a princess, and can be alone with your thoughts. It also has to be a space where you can study and prepare yourself to face your day. The only word that really describes it is "sanctuary"; your room has to be your sanctuary.

I hope that when you look at the rooms on the following pages, you are inspired to make your room a wonderful place. Don't think that you have to do everything exactly the same as I did. Don't even think that you have to use the same colors or materials. Let your creative minds explode— use something from each of the rooms if you want. Trust me, there are no rules in creating your own Cool Room.

One more thing, my friends: I'm always around to answer your room decorating questions, so email me anytime at **MarkMontanoNYC@aol.com.**

Much love and creativity to you all!
Mark

COSMO*girl* cool room

royal treatment

Style guru Mark Montano gave this room a serious style upgrade to make it fit for a queen! Mark decided that a sophisticated color scheme and luxurious accessories would give it a mature look. First he painted the walls a rich cream color, then he added wide olive stripes and thin orange ones to give the illusion of more space. Elegant silk storage boxes organize things, and a beaded velvet ottoman adds a regal touch. Mark finished off the room by making beautiful drapes for the windows and padded pillows to hang on the wall alongside the bed. A gold chair and mirrors (we got ours at a thrift store) add extra glamour to the room.

turn the page to make it yourself

tray station table

Supplies
- **TV tray table**
- **3 yards of brocade fabric**
- **8 pieces of ½-inch-wide velvet ribbon, cut 12 inches long**
- **straight pins**
- **scissors**
- **needle and thread**

1. Drape fabric over the open TV tray. Cut the bottom so the fabric just hits the floor. Hem the bottom.
2. Pinch each corner 3 inches down from the tabletop to form a fold. Pin the sides of the fold together, tucking in any fullness. Repeat another 3 inches down on all corners.
3. Tie the pieces of ribbon into neat bows.
4. Take the fabric off the table and hand stitch closed each pinned fold. Stitch one bow over each closure.
5. Remove the pins and replace the cloth on the TV tray.

queen bead candle

Supplies
- **tall glass pillar-candle holder**
- **3-yard strand of small pearl beads**
- **hot-glue gun and glue sticks**
- **household adhesive**
- **tall pillar candle**

1. Start at the very top of the glass holder and carefully hot-glue one end of the string of beads to the glass.
2. Slowly and neatly wrap the beads around the holder, hot-gluing then pressing them down as you go. You can wrap the rows close together to cover all of the glass or leave space between rows to let the glass peek out.
3. At the bottom of the glass holder, snip off any excess beads; hot-glue the end securely to the glass.
4. When dry, place a dab of household adhesive on the top and the bottom ends to make them extra secure. Place a candle in the holder and display.

NOTE: Never leave a lit candle unattended!

chips ahoy! wall art

Supplies (for one picture)
- **8-by-16-inch pop-out frame with white mat**
- **24 paint chips in complementing colors**
- **white craft glue**
- **5 sheets white construction paper**
- **gold spray paint**
- **scissors**
- **newspaper**

1. Cut the paint chips into twenty-four 1-inch squares.
2. Cut the white paper into twenty-four ½-inch squares. Place them on newspaper in a well-ventilated area and spray them with gold paint. Let dry for 3 hours.
3. Open the frame and lay the paint chip squares on the white mat in a pattern you like (try 8 rows of 3 squares, like ours).
4. Glue down the paint chips. Let dry for 2 hours. Glue a gold square in the center of each chip. Let dry. Reframe and hang up.

film fanatic

Quiet on the set! Learn how to make your room cooler than the director's cut of *Donnie Darko*. Foreign film posters add a graphic, cinematic flair. Painting one whole wall red-carpet red makes it really pop between two white walls.

FEDERICO FELLINI
LA DOLCE VITA
MARCELLO MASTROIANNI · ANITA EKBERG
TOTALSCOPE

turn the page to make it yourself

personalized director's chair

Supplies
- **director's chair**
- **white pencil**
- **ruler**
- **fabric glue**
- **tweezers**
- **1-2 bags of ¼-inch rhinestones**

1. Remove the panel from the back of the chair and lay it flat.
2. Sketch your name in white pencil—use a ruler to draw top and bottom guidelines so the letters are even.
3. Put a dab of fabric glue on the back of each rhinestone.
4. Use tweezers to place the rhinestones on a letter. Repeat to cover the whole name in rhinestones.
5. Let dry completely. Replace the panel.

film-strip artwork

Supplies
- **35-millimeter camera with film (not a digital camera)**
- **double-sided tape**

1. Take pictures of anything—your friends, family, pets. They should either be all vertical or all horizontal.
2. Develop the film and pick your 3 favorite images.
3. Take the negatives to a film lab and ask them to print each frame as an 11-by-14-inch print, keeping in the film bracket borders.
4. Hang the prints in a row on your wall with double-sided tape.

living room chic!

Want to make your bedroom a cool hangout for your friends? Here's how.

Pick two or three colors in a related tone for a chic look. We used golds, oranges, and browns. Turn your bed into a "sofa" with bolster pillows and square wall pads. Use one bold piece, like a mirror over the bed, as a main focal point. Arrange a comfy chair and a big table in front of the "sofa" to form a conversation pit, where everyone can relax.

turn the page to make it yourself ➡

plaid lantern

Supplies (to make one lantern)
- **two 12-inch-high plain lamp shades**
- **2 yards of plaid cotton fabric**
- **4 yards of ½-inch-wide satin ribbon**
- **hot-glue gun and glue sticks**
- **spray adhesive**
- **light socket with cord**
- **40-watt bulb**
- **S-hook**
- **scissors**

1. Lay the fabric down with the wrong side facing up.
2. In a well-ventilated area, spray one shade all over with adhesive. Lay the shade at the edge of the fabric and carefully roll it to cover it completely with fabric.
3. Cut off the extra fabric on top, bottom, and where the two ends meet.
4. Hot-glue the ribbon around the top edges.

5. Repeat the process with the other lamp shade.

6. Screw the bulb into the socket. Pull the cord through the top of one lamp shade.

7. Neatly hot-glue the bases of the lamp shades together to form a big lantern.

8. Hot-glue the ribbon around the middle to cover the seam.

9. Screw the S-hook into the ceiling and hang the lantern from it. Plug the cord into an electrical socket.

storage ottoman

Supplies
- **2 identical trunks, 12-by-32-inches or smaller**
- **4 yards of 60-inch-wide dark orange velour fabric**
- **32-inch square of 3-inch-thick foam**
- **scissors**
- **Velcro strips**

1. Cut a 36-inch square from the velour. Center it on the foam square; fold down the sides and fold the edges over in back. Hot-glue in place to create the top cushion.
2. Measure the height and width of the front of one trunk and of one side of both trunks put together. (Ours were both 12-by-32 inches.) Add ½ inch to all sides and cut 4 velour rectangles to those measurements. Stitch ½-inch hems on all 4 edges of the 4 panels.
3. Adhere the Velcro strips along the inside edges of all the panels, then along the edges of the sides of the trunks. Attach the panels to the trunks.
4. Attach the cushion to the top of the trunks with Velcro so you can remove it to store stuff inside.

square wall pads

Supplies (for 3 pads)
- **three 25-inch squares of ½-inch-thick plywood (hardware stores will cut for a fee)**
- **3 yards of dark orange velour fabric, cut into 3 equal pieces**
- **3 yards of quilter's batting, cut into 3 equal pieces**
- **staple gun and staples**
- **3 wire-backed picture-hanger sets**
- **hammer and nails**

1. Center batting on each wood square; fold edges over in back and staple them down. (Don't cover back of square.)

2. Repeat the process with velour.

3. On the back of each square, attach a picture hanger centered 2 inches down from top. Hang the squares next to each other on the wall behind the bed.

bolster pillows

Supplies (to make one pillow)
- **6-by-36-inch round foam bolster insert**
- **1 ½ yards of light orange velour or cotton velvet fabric**
- **scissors**
- **straight pins**
- **needle and thread**

1. Cut a 38-by-16-inch velour rectangle. Fold it lengthwise, with velour facing in.
2. Stitch the open long side 15 inches in from each end, leaving an 8-inch opening in the center of the seam.
3. Trace the round end of the bolster onto the remaining fabric twice; add 1 inch all the way around the circles. Cut out circles.
4. With all velour facing in, pin one circle to each end of the tube. Neatly stitch the circles to the tube with 1-inch seams to form the ends of the bolster case. Go slowly so the fabric will gather as you go along.
5. Remove the pins. Turn the bolster case right-side out through the hole in the center of the seam.
6. Insert the foam bolster through the hole.
7. Hand stitch the opening closed.

it's eclectic!

Make your room as multi-faceted as your personality. Mark brought together an array of interesting "found objects" that complement each other in an organized-chaos kind of way! First he painted the walls a flat latex Tequila Lime. Next he hung floor-to-ceiling patterned drapes on the windows to give the illusion of a taller space. A bronze fish statue gives the room a touch of fun. A solid-color fringed throw and striped pillows, plus an intricate bedspread, add to the mixed-pattern vibe. Pretty white silk orchids and a frosty vase blend well with a black-and-white fashion collage (see page 39). Shelves made from fish tanks (shown on page 41) are perfect to show off your stuff.

turn the page to make it yourself

about face wall art

Supplies
- **camera**
- **very small, sharp scissors (try staight manicure scissors)**
- **newspaper**
- **black spray paint**
- **black picture frames**
- **white cardstock or posterboard**

1. To create these silhouettes, have your friends and family (and yourself!) stand against a white wall and take a bunch of close-up profile shots.
2. Print 4-by-6-inch photos, pick your favorites, and cut out each person's profile.
3. Bring the cutouts outside, lay them flat on newspaper, and spray-paint them black.
4. Let them dry completely and then frame them against a white background.

collage bound

Supplies
- **double-sided tape**
- **twelve 12-inch-square cork tiles**
- **fashion magazines or books**
- **push pins**
- **black picture frames**

1. Using double-sided tape, mount the cork tiles on the wall in 3 rows of 4 tiles each to make a corkboard.
2. Photocopy fashion images from the magazine in color or black and white.
3. Pin the photos onto the corkboard to form a collage.
4. Save your favorite pictures to put in the black frames and display them around your room or on a table.

tanks a lot! shelf unit

Supplies
- **three 10-gallon glass fish tanks**
- **1-by-12-inch pine board, cut to custom length**
- **five 8-inch-long pieces of 2-by-4-inch wood**
- **hammer and nails**
- **black paint and paintbrush**
- **fluorescent under-cabinet light**

1. Place the tanks end-to-end and measure the length. (Ours was 60 inches.)
2. Have a 1-by-12-inch pine board cut to this length.
3. Nail an 8-inch-long piece of wood to each corner of the board and one in the center to create a bench-like table.
4. Paint the table black. When it's dry, place the tanks on the table, in a row, on their sides, so the open part is facing you.
5. Place the light in the center tank and plug it in.

shell shock

Supplies
- **assorted seashells**
- **gold enamel spray paint**
- **newspaper**

1. Collect a bunch of seashells or buy a big bag of them.
2. Bring the seashells outside, lay them on newspaper, and spray-paint them with gold enamel to accentuate their interesting grooves.
3. Let the shells dry, then place them on display!

room for two

Sharing a bathroom with your sister or a roommate? Mark has some great solutions for keeping things neat *and* cute.

Decide on two coordinating colors (one for you, one for her) for everything from your towels to your toothbrushes, so you always know what's yours and what's hers. Keep your toiletries in portable bins stowed under the sink, so you can bring them to your room if she's hogging the bathroom! Put pockets on your shower curtain for extra storage rather than cluttering up your countertop.

turn the page to make it yourself

aprés-bath towel robe

Supplies
- **2 bath towels**
- **sewing machine**
- **scissors**
- **needle and thread**
- **hook-and-eye fastener**

1. Place the towels together with the color you want on the outside of the robe facing in. Machine stitch one long side together with a ½-inch seam.

2. Fold the now-stitched towels in half lengthwise. Starting from the stitched side, sew 12 inches of the top edges together with a ½-inch seam.

3. Seven inches in and down from the stitched sides of robe, cut out a 6-inch circle on both sides. Zigzag-stitch around the openings to keep them from unrave›ling.

4. Flip the robe right-side out, slip your arms through the holes, and close one side over the other. Sew on a hook and eye 1 inch in from the edges to close flap.

silky sink curtain

Supplies
- **2 yards of blue nylon fabric**
- **2 yards of blue ribbon**
- **Velcro tape**
- **sewing machine**
- **scissors**
- **needle and thread**

1. Wrap the fabric all the way around the top edge of sink. Measure this length, then add half that number to it. (Our sink was 44 inches around, so we added 22 inches.) Cut a piece of fabric the length of the combined numbers. Measure the height of the sink from floor to rim. Cut the bottom edge of the fabric to fit this height.

2. Machine-sew ½-inch hems on all sides. Neatly stitch the ribbon to the entire top edge of the skirt, gathering the fabric as you go. Cut off any excess ribbon when you get to the end.

3. Place the Velcro tape all along the rim of the sink and along the back edge of the fabric where the ribbon is stitched to the skirt.

4. Attach the skirt evenly around the sink.

dot's-dot trash can

Supplies
- **a white frosted plastic trash can**
- **color-coded office dot stickers**
- **1-inch-wide paintbrush**
- **decoupage glue**

1. Wipe the can with a wet cloth and dry it well.
Stick different-colored dots all over the can to
create a random, fun pattern that you like. (We
used blue and green dots of different sizes.)
2. With the paintbrush, carefully and evenly go over
the entire can with a thin layer of decoupage glue.
(This keeps the dots on even when the bathroom
gets steamy!)
3. Let the glue dry for 2 hours.

pretty pocket shower curtain

Supplies
- **2½ yards each of blue and green nylon fabric**
- **½ yard of dark teal nylon fabric**
- **12 shower curtain rings**
- **12 silk flowers**
- **sewing machine**
- **hot-glue gun and glue sticks**
- **scissors**
- **thread**

1. Cut two 36-by-72-inch panels, one from blue and one from green fabric. Place them together, right-sides in, and machine stitch one long side together to form curtain. Sew ½-inch hems on all sides.
2. Cut three 10-by-10-inch squares from leftover fabric of each color. Stitch the pocket squares to the front of the curtain wherever you like, leaving the top open.
3. Stencil both of your initials on the teal fabric, then cut them out. Hot-glue the letters onto the front of the curtain. Cut twelve 1-inch-long slits 1 inch down from the top of the curtain and spaced 6 inches apart, for rings.
4. Cut the stems off the flowers. Hot-glue one flower to each curtain ring.

cool room?
cool walls!

Here are Mark's tips on how to paint like a pro:

- To get the base color on smoothly, roll a big W on the wall. Go over it several times, moving a little at a time to fill in the spaces. Then repeat with a larger W until the wall is covered.
- Busy patterns like these look best when used in small areas, so try them on just one wall or on a closet door.
- Practice makes perfect! Before painting it on your wall, try using each technique on scrap paper until you like the results.

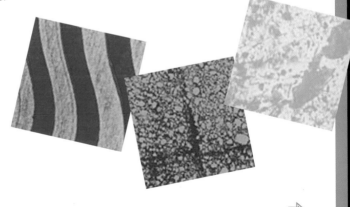

turn the page to make it yourself ▶

sponge painting

Supplies
- **2 shades of latex paint in the same color family (one light, one dark)**
- **paint tray**
- **9-inch paint roller and foam cover**
- **paint edger**
- **newspaper**
- **3-by-4-inch sponge**

1. Lay down newspaper under the wall you're going to paint. Paint the whole wall in the light color using the roller. Use the edger to do the corners and edges. Let dry overnight.

2. Dip one side of the sponge into the dark paint. Gently press the sponge on newspaper to remove excess paint. Line up the sponge

vertically with the top right corner of the wall and stamp, going down the wall in a straight line. Redip the sponge and blot as needed (every 4 stamps or so).

3. Continue going down the wall in even vertical rows, one right next to the other, until you've finished painting the whole area.

squeegee painting

Supplies
- **craft knife and blades**
- **2 shades of latex paint in the same color family (one light, one dark)**
- **paint tray**
- **9-inch paint roller and foam cover**
- **paint edger**
- **squeegee**
- **newspaper**

1. Lay down newspaper under the wall you're going to paint. Paint the wall in the light color using the roller. Use the edger to do the corners and edges. Let dry overnight.

2. Use craft knife to carefully cut out a ½-inch-wide space from the rubber strip of the squeegee every ½ inch along the entire length.

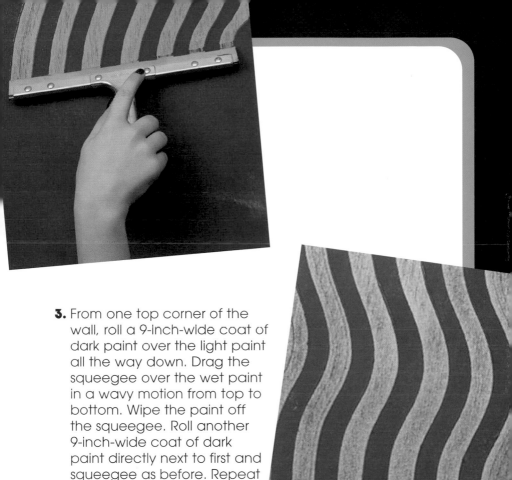

3. From one top corner of the wall, roll a 9-inch-wide coat of dark paint over the light paint all the way down. Drag the squeegee over the wet paint in a wavy motion from top to bottom. Wipe the paint off the squeegee. Roll another 9-inch-wide coat of dark paint directly next to first and squeegee as before. Repeat until the wall is done.

bag painting

Supplies
- **2 shades of latex paint in same color family (one light, one dark)**
- **paint tray**
- **9-inch paint roller and foam cover**
- **paint edger**
- **medium plastic bag**
- **newspaper**

1. Lay down newspaper under the wall you're going to paint. Paint the wall in the light color using the roller. Use the edger to do the corners and edges. Let dry overnight.

2. Mix the dark paint with water—½ cup of water per each pint of paint. Tightly scrunch up the plastic bag. Dip the bottom of the bag in the paint. Press the bag on newspaper to blot off the excess paint. Press the crinkled bag firmly on any part of the wall and carefully lift it off.

3. Continue pressing and lifting the bag to create a mottled effect—make sure not to press in the same area more than once. Redip the bag and blot as needed (every 4 presses or so) until the wall is covered.

asian fusion

Mark mixed in a little bit of this and that to give this room some real Eastern spice! To get this sophisticated, Pan-Asian look, Mark first striped the walls in sweet colors that match the bedding. Next he hung bamboo lattices to frame the bed. Delicate silk flowers in glass vases and a silk bonsai tree (of course!) add to the Far East appeal of the room. Mark made the bed blossom with this bright floral-print motif. Bright paper lanterns add color to the room and give it a pretty Asian-garden feeling.

turn the page to make it yourself

chopstick lamp

Supplies (for one lamp)
- **pack of 8-inch wooden chopsticks**
- **wood glue**
- **8 inches of 20-gauge wire**
- **light socket with cord**
- **15-watt bulb (higher watt bulbs can cause wood to burn)**

1. Lay 2 pairs of chopsticks parallel on a table, 6 inches apart, wide side down (don't break them apart!). Place 2 more pairs perpendicular to the first two and 1 inch in from ends. Glue to form a square.
2. Repeat, adding pairs of chopsticks log cabin-style to make a 10-inch-tall shade.
3. String the wire across the inside of the shade 4 chopsticks from top, and twist the ends around the sticks to secure.
4. Feed the light socket up from the shade's open bottom and loop the cord around the wire so the socket dangles in the middle. Add bulb. Voilà!

NOTE: Never leave light on unattended!
CAUTION: Higher watt bulbs can cause chopstick to burn

wall flowers

Supplies (for one picture)
- **printed origami paper**
- **glue stick**
- **scissors**
- **8-by-10-inch frame with mat**

1. Pick 2 pieces of printed origami paper in colors that match your walls (but not each other—a little clashing is good!).
2. Enlarge each piece to 8½-by-11 inches on a color copier.
3. Use one piece as the base: Trim 3 inches from the length of the base paper. From the other piece cut a big flower freehand (uneven is funky!) and glue it onto the center of the base paper.
4. Center your art in the frame so 1 inch of the mat shows on the top and the bottom.
5. Replace the glass, then hang the frame on the wall.
6. Repeat with different papers to create a series, as shown.

ottoman empire

Supplies
- **2-by-2-foot piece of 1-inch-thick plywood**
- **kit of 4 cabinet legs with attachment**
- **2-by-2-foot piece of foam, 7 inches thick**
- **1½ yards of cotton fabric**
- **3 yards of fringe to match the fabric**
- **hot-glue gun and glue sticks**
- **staple gun and staples**

1. Attach the cabinet legs to the bottom of the plywood, following the instructions in the kit. The legs should be placed 1 inch in from each corner of the wood.
2. Cover the top of the plywood with glue. Attach the foam.
3. Drape the fabric over the foam and neatly fold in the corners. Staple the fabric to the plywood underneath under the seat, all the way around. Hot-glue the fringe around the bottom edges of the plywood.

70 split personality

split personality

What if your roommate is the complete opposite of you? Here's how to combine two different styles—and still make your room look good. These tips will work whether you share a room with a stranger or a sister!

1. Start by talking to your roommate (or your sister) about your style likes and dislikes before you go shopping for room stuff.
2. Negotiate the items each of you can't live without and the ones you can compromise on. (You don't really need all 50 pictures of your celeb crush—you can live with just 3 or 4, right? Right!)
3. Find a theme that you can interpret for each style, like flowers. We blended girlie daisies with dark red rock-star roses.
4. To separate the sides of your room visually, put curtains with different fabrics on each side of the window (roomies each buy an extra flat bedsheet).
5. Arranging things symmetrically helps different styles look better together, so position similar items in the same place on both sides of the room. Put chairs at the foot of each bed, dressers between the beds, and mirrors over each bed.

turn the page to make it yourself

chalkboards

Whether you or your roommate are opposites or more like twins, these boards are great ways to keep track of your busy schedules.

Supplies (for one board)
- **8-by-1-foot piece of ½-inch-thick plywood**
- **3 cups acrylic paint in any color you like**
- **1½ cups water-based glazing medium**
- **½ cup powdered tile grout**
- **2-inch paintbrush**
- **6 yards of faux flower vines**
- **fine-grain sandpaper**
- **chalk**
- **staple gun and staples**

1. Sand the edges and the front of the board until all are smooth.
2. Mix together the paint, glazing medium, and powdered grout until well blended to create the chalkboard paint. Using the paintbrush, cover the entire front of the board evenly with the thick mixture. Let dry overnight. Gently sand over the paint. Wipe away the excess dust. Apply a second coat of the mixture. Let dry and gently sand again.
3. Wipe the board with a soft, damp cloth until clean. Staple the vines around the edges to form a frame. Prop the board against the wall.

flower garland

Supplies
- **2 ½ yards each of rose and daisy vines or faux flower vines of your choice**
- **temporary mounting putty**

1. Measure the height of one side of your window and half of its width. Twist together the ends of the rose vines to make one long vine that will fit the combined measurement of this space. Repeat with the daisy vines.
2. Twist together one end of the daisy vine with one end of the rose vine to create one long, continuous vine. Drape it over the top of the window and tuck it around the curtain rod, letting the ends hang down.
3. Secure the vines to the window frame with mounting putty, which won't ruin the wall.

stenciled dressers

Supplies (for one dresser)
- **5-drawer lingerie chest**
- **assorted colors of high-gloss spray paint**
- **stencils**
- **screwdriver or masking tape**

1. Remove drawers from chest. Remove the drawer pulls with a screwdriver or cover them with masking tape. Tape a stencil on one drawer front. In a ventilated area, spray-paint over it. Neatly peel back stencil to reveal design.
2. Continue with the other drawers. Spray-paint some of them a solid color so the stenciled ones really pop. Let drawers dry at least 2 hours.
3. Put the drawer pulls back on with the screwdriver or remove the masking tape and return the drawers to the dresser.

room divider

Supplies:
- metal- or wood-framed 3-panel room divider
- six 9-to-15-inch-long tension rods
- 3 flat twin-size sheets (choose ones that complement your bedding)
- sewing machine
- scissors
- needle and thread

1. Carefully remove the original fabric from the divider.

2. Measure the length and the width of one panel in the divider. Add 5 inches to the width and 4 inches to the length. Cut a fabric panel of this size from a flat sheet.

3. Machine stitch a ½-inch hem on both long sides. Fold down a 2-inch flap along one short edge and stitch it down to create a tube for the tension rod. Repeat on the other short edge.

4. Repeat with the remaining 2 sheets.

5. Insert the tension rods into both tubes of one panel. Gather the fabric along the rods. Tighten the rods until panel hangs neatly in the frame. Repeat with the other 2 panels.

clean up your closet!

You can have a closet that's as glam as any Hollywood celeb's. Here are Mark's tips to recreate their fabulous space:

- Remove the closet doors (ask Mom or Dad for help), put up curtains, and add carpet to make it feel like a luxurious dressing area.
- Paint the inside of the closet a color you love.
- Hot-glue fringe to the edge of your shelves as an extra touch.
- Photograph your shoes and tape the pix to the boxes, so you can keep the shoes protected but still quickly find what you need in the morning when you're getting dressed.
- Use stacking baskets for loose items like bags, socks, tights, undies, and bras.

turn the page to make it yourself

pom-pom curtains

Supplies

- moiré fabric (measure your closet doors from top to bottom, double it, and then add another 10 inches)
- 10 yards of pom-pom trim
- 1 yard of fringe trim
- tension rod to fit across your closet
- sewing machine
- scissors
- needle and thread

1. Cut the fabric in half widthwise to get 2 equal-sized panels. Neatly stitch a ½-inch hem around the 4 sides of each panel.

2. Fold down a short end of each panel 3 inches and stitch it along the bottom to create a sleeve for the rod.

3. Stitch the pom-pom trim along the sides and bottom of each panel.

4. Slide each panel onto the tension rod. Expand the rod until it fits snugly across the top of the closet.

5. Tie the curtains back with fringe trim or let them hang loose to hide your stuff!

jewelry organizer

Supplies
- **old wooden frame**
- **gold spray paint**
- **roll of small mesh window screening**
- **scissors**
- **heavy-duty staple gun and staples**

1. Remove the glass and backing from the frame. Spray-paint it gold (in the garage or outside) Let dry 2 hours.
2. Cut a piece of mesh that fits into the frame plus an extra inch on all 4 sides. Staple the mesh around all 4 edges of the frame back.
3. Hang or prop up the frame inside your closet. Then hook all your earrings into the holes in the mesh.

fabric-covered hanger

Supplies (for one hanger)
- **wooden suit hanger with pants bar**
- **½ yard of moiré fabric**
- **½ yard of 1-inch-wide satin ribbon**
- **sewing machine**
- **scissors**
- **pencil**
- **needle and thread**
- **hot-glue gun and glue sticks**

1. Lay the hanger on the fabric. Trace around the hanger to create a pattern. Then add ¾ inch to slanted sides and 2 inches to straight bottom side. Cut out. Repeat so you have two equal-sized pieces.
2. Machine-stitch the shiny sides together ½ inch in from edges of the slanted sides. Leave a ¼ inch opening at the tip of the triangle for the hanger to fit through.
3. Turn the fabric right-side out. Slip it onto the hanger. Fold the bottom edges under and carefully hot-glue the sides closed.
4. Tie the ribbon into a bow on the hook of the hanger.

storage box

Supplies
- **medium cardboard box (try a large shoebox or a round hatbox)**
- **1 yard of moiré fabric**
- **2 yards of fringe trim**
- **hot-glue gun and glue sticks**
- **scissors**

1. Lay the fabric out with the shiny side facedown. Place the bottom of the box on the fabric. Wrap the outside of the box just like you would a present, neatly folding the edges up over the sides of the box.
2. Hot-glue the fabric in place inside the box. Trim any excess fabric.
3. Repeat the wrapping process with the top of the box, again neatly folding the edges over into the inside cover. Hot-glue the fabric in place. Trim any excess fabric.
4. Using one continuous piece of fringe trim, neatly hot-glue it around the edges of the box top. Overlap ½ inch of fringe where 2 ends meet. Cut off excess. Glue down end.

citrus blast

Thanks to Mark, this room now has more zing than a glass of OJ! Instead of an ultra girly room, this fruit-juicy color scheme is sunny and bright. Eye-popping accents like an orange lampshade and green curtains are set off by clean eggshell walls. For some mod sophistication Mark added a clear table and a shaggy rug. How sub-*lime*!

turn the page to make it yourself

colorful reflection hanging mirror

Supplies (for one painting)
- **nine 12-by-12-inch square mirror tiles**
- **thin-point permanent marker**
- **2 colors of high-gloss enamel paint**
- **paintbrush**
- **heavy-duty mounting tape**

1. With the marker, draw a circle on each mirror, at least 1 inch in from all sides. Use a compass or trace a 10-inch cake pan.
2. Paint the outer edges of the mirrors, leaving the circles unpainted. Paint 5 of the tiles pink and 4 lavender. Let dry overnight.
3. Attach the mirrors to the wall with the mounting tape. Make 3 rows of 3 tiles each, in alternating colors, to form a square.

citrus blast 89

clear factor wall art

Supplies
- **18-by-24-inch Lucite box frame**
- **3 colors of high-gloss latex paint**
- **newspaper**
- **measuring cup with spout**
- **hammer and nail**

1. Remove the frame's backing and mat. Place the frame facedown on the newspaper.
2. Measure ½ cup of paint; drizzle it in large loops on the inside of the frame. Let dry overnight.
3. Repeat with the next paint color, drizzling it over the previous color. Let dry overnight.
4. Repeat with the third color. When the paint is totally dry, flip the frame over and replace the backing. Hang it gently from a nail in the wall.

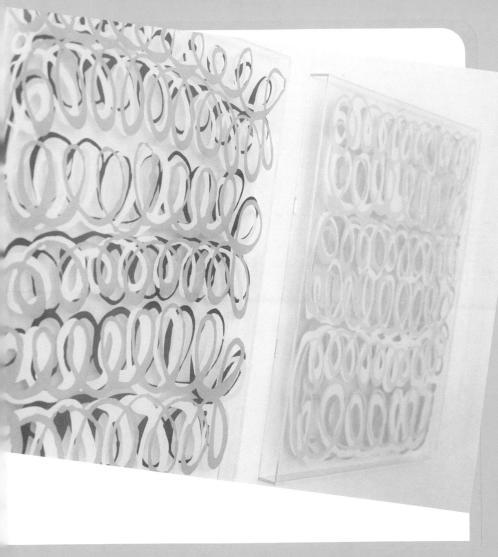

pom-pom girl pillows

Supplies (for one circle pillow)
- **2 yards of satin fabric**
- **spool of matching thread**
- **quilter's batting**
- **ball of yarn in a color that contrasts with the fabric**
- **2 pieces of cardboard**
- **sewing machine**

1. From the satin fabric, cut out two 18-inch circles and a strip 4 inches wide and 56½ inches long. For square pillows start with two 18-inch squares.
2. With the shiny edges facing each other, hand-stitch a long edge of the strip to the edge of the circle, gathering the fabric as you go. Leave 2 inches unsewn at the end so you can add the batting. Sew the other edge of the strip to the edge of the other circle in the same way. (In the end, the pillow casing should look like a little tire.)
3. Turn it right-side out. Stuff with batting and stitch up the hole.
4. To make pom-poms, cut a rectangular piece of cardboard twice as long as you want your pom-pom to be (for a pom-pom that's 2 inches in diameter, make your cardboard 4 inches long).

Wrap your yarn neatly, end-to-end around the card-board until it's as thick as you want your pom-pom to be. Cut the yarn. Cut one more piece of yarn the same length as your cardboard, slide it through between the cardboard and the yarn, and pull it to one end. Then tie the cut piece of yarn tightly into a knot around the wrapped ends.

With sharp scissors, cut the opposite wrapped ends. Fluff the yarn into a round pom-pom and trim any strays.

5. Stitch the pom-pom to the center of the pillow.

photo credits

Everett Collection: 21 (right)
Douglas Friedman: 20, 21 (left), 23 (left), 25, 42
Getty Images: 23 (right)
Tria Giovan: 34, 37, 39, 41, 43, 86, 87, 89, 91, 93
Andrew McCaul: 26, 27, 29, 31 - 33, 37, 44, 49, 51, 53 – 61, 70, 72 – 78, 81 - 83, 85
Matt Rodgers: 12, 15, 17, 19, 62, 63, 65, 67, 69

index

More cool DIY...

50 Ways to Get the Look:
Amazing Clothes, Bags, Hair
Treatments & More.

978-1-58816-624-1 / $7.95